AT
ZOO

WRITTEN BY
Andrea Butler

ILLUSTRATED BY
John Sandford

ScottForesman

A Division of HarperCollinsPublishers

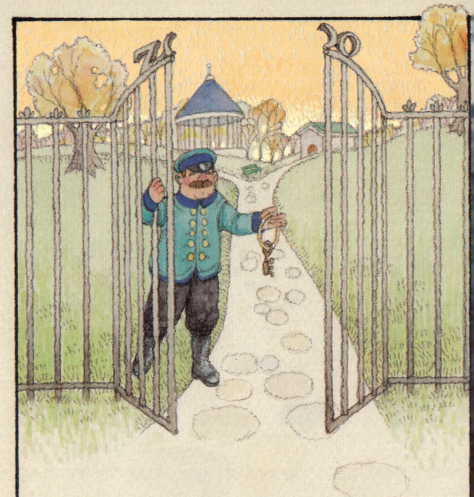

What can you see at the zoo?

Six monkeys
swing, swing, swinging.

Five tigers
claw, claw, clawing.

4

Four elephants
stomp, stomp, stomping.

Three lions
roar, roar, roaring.

6

Two bears
doze, doze, dozing.

One zoo
close, close, closing.